My Parents' Divorce

Designed and produced by
Aladdin Books Ltd

First published in 2009
in the United States
by Stargazer Books,
distributed by
Black Rabbit Books
PO Box 3263
Mankato, MN 56002

4/09 Creative Co. 27.10
Illustrator: Christopher O'Neill

The author, Julia Cole, is a trained counsellor and one of the UK's best-known
relationship experts. She writes and broadcasts regularly on relationship issues.

Printed in the United States

Library of Congress Cataloging-in-Publication Data

Cole, Julia.
  My parents' divorce / Julia Cole. -- 2nd ed.
      p. cm. -- (Thoughts and feelings)
  Includes index.
  ISBN 978-1-59604-169-1
  1. Children of divorced parents--Psychology--Juvenile literature. 2. Divorce--Juvenile literature. I. Title.
  HQ777.5.C635 2009
  306.89--dc22
                                        2008022466

My Parents' Divorce

Julia Cole

Stargazer Books
Mankato, Minnesota

Contents

What Is Divorce? 6

What Happens? 9

Why Does It Happen? 14

Difficult Feelings 19

Feeling OK 24

Don't Forget 28

Find Out More 30

Index 32

Introduction

The children in this book know how it feels when a mom and dad decide to live apart. You may have a friend whose parents are separated or divorced, or your parents may have split up. Join the children in this book as they talk about their feelings.

I live with my mom and see my dad at weekends.

My mom and dad are separated. I live with my dad.

My parents are getting a divorce.

Mom and Dad divorced when I was a baby. I live with my mom, but I see my dad all the time.

What Is Divorce?

Adam is explaining to Leon that separation is when two grown-ups who have lived together decide to live apart. If they are married they may also decide to get a divorce. You may hear someone say that his or her parents have split up. This can mean that they are separated or divorced.

Splitting up is when parents separate. It's also when parents divorce.

> What is the difference between divorce and separation?

> Grown-ups can only divorce if they are married. They may separate first.

▶ Splitting Up

Splitting up is when grown-ups decide to live apart. If they are married, they may decide to divorce. Grown-ups who split up usually live in separate homes. They may live alone or they may live with a new partner.

◀ Who Gets Divorced?

Only grown-ups who have been married can get a divorce, because a divorce is a legal end to a marriage. But grown-ups who are married can still separate without getting a divorce. However, even though parents are divorcing each other, they are *not* divorcing their children.

▶ A Hard Decision

It's not easy for a husband and wife to decide to end their marriage. They may spend a long time trying to solve their problems before they realize they just can't fix them.

If parents have been fighting a lot, some children may even feel relieved that they are divorcing.

Adam, tell us about your parents.

"My parents split up about four years ago. I don't see my dad anymore. I live with my mom. Because my mom and dad never married, they didn't need to get a divorce. I don't think it matters if you call it divorce, separation, or splitting up. They all mean that two grown-ups have decided to live separately."

What Happens?

My dad is looking for somewhere else to live.

Dad and I moved to a new house.

We've decided to live apart.

One parent usually moves out.

You don't have to split up!

Alice is telling Lily that her dad is going to live somewhere else. When Lily's parents split up, she and her dad moved out. Each situation is different, but most moms and dads want to make sure their children will be OK. Whatever your mom and dad do, you will still be looked after.

Story: Staying Friends

1 Saba thought divorce or separation happened right away.

2 Josie thought Saba would forget her. But he wanted to stay friends.

3 Talking helped Josie and Saba to realize that each situation is different.

Why is it different for Saba and Josie?

Saba and Josie now know that every family is different. One parent may move out before you have been told what is happening. Or your parents may tell you that they are splitting up before anything happens. Like Saba you may stay in your home, or like Josie you may have to move house.

▶ What About Me?

Sometimes your parents will decide between themselves whom you stay with or they may ask you what you think. Sometimes the courts need to help decide this. They may also decide when and if you see your other parent.

Can he live with us in our new house?

◀ Together Again!

The parent from whom you live apart may try to visit or to see you as much as he or she can. However, this may not always be possible. You can ask the parent with whom you live to explain the new situation.

▶ A Parent Forever

After your parents divorce you will usually live with only one parent for most of the time. But the parent who lives somewhere else is still your mom or dad. They won't stop loving you.

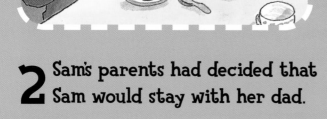

Story: Does She Love Me?

1 Sam wanted her mom and dad to stay together, but her mom was moving out.

2 Sam's parents had decided that Sam would stay with her dad.

3 Sam found it difficult to understand how her mom could leave and still love her.

Will Sam's mom still love her?

Sam's mom is going to live apart from Sam and her dad, but this doesn't mean that she will stop loving Sam. She will still see Sam regularly. Some parents stay in contact with their children a lot. Others don't visit very much, but whatever happens, they will always be your mom and dad.

Alice, you live with your dad now. Do you see your mom?
"Yes. When my parents separated they decided that my sister, Nicole, and I should live with Dad. We moved to a new house and everything. But Nicole and I still see Mom on weekends and during vacations."

Why Does It Happen?

Kieron is telling his sister Holly why he thinks that their parents are splitting up. There can be lots of reasons why parents split up. They may not love each other in the same way as they used to, or they may meet someone else they want to be with. Whatever the reason, it doesn't mean that they will stop loving you.

Why do they argue all the time?

It's just that Mom and Dad don't love each other like they used to.

But why not? It's not fair. I still love them the same.

▶ Arguing Again!

Parents can argue so much they become very unhappy. They may feel that they should part in order to stop the fights. They may decide that even though divorce or separation is upsetting, in the end it will mean that everyone can be happier.

It's quieter here than at home!

◀ New Partners

One parent may find a new friend they can talk to and get along with better. He or she may choose to live with them instead of your mom or dad. If this happens, you may feel very angry toward your parent's new partner.

▶ Mom Still Loves Him

Sometimes only one parent wants to live away from the other parent. If this is the case, the parent who doesn't want the other one to leave may find it difficult to accept and understand the new situation.

Story: It's Not Your Fault

1 Jo and Jim Jones were arguing over a computer game.

2 Their mom heard them arguing. She came in and told them off.

3 A week later, Mr. and Mrs. Jones told Jo and Jim that they were splitting up.

Are Mr. and Mrs. Jones splitting up because Jo and Jim argued?

No, definitely not. Parents who split up do so because they feel unhappy with each other. Mrs. Jones was cross with Jim and Jo, but it had nothing to do with the decision to separate from Mr. Jones. It is important to remember that you are not to blame for the separation or divorce of your parents.

▶ Who's To Blame?

You may want to blame one of your parents if they split up. But grown-ups often decide together to separate or divorce. Even if it is just one parent's choice, blaming him or her won't help anyone.

▼ I Don't Understand

Sometimes the situation may be very complicated. If you can, try talking to an older brother, sister, or grandparent to help you to understand better what is happening.

Is it Mom's fault for working too hard?

...or Dad's for playing so much golf?

Kieron, do you understand why your parents are getting a divorce?

"Holly says it's Mom's fault for shouting at Dad. But it's not fair to blame Mom. Dad shouts at Mom, too. I think they are splitting up because they will be happier if they don't live together. I'll miss Dad but it will be better if the fights stop."

Difficult Feelings

Gabriela is over at Carla's house after school. She is asking Carla how she felt when her parents split up. Like Gabriela and Carla, you might have lots of difficult and confusing feelings if your parents separate or get a divorce.

I hate you!

You may feel very angry.

I got upset when people said nasty things about my mom.

I still feel mad at my mom.

19

▶ But I Want Them Both

You may feel upset and want your mom and dad to stay together, even if they have been sad. You may feel angry with the parent with whom you live and want to blame him or her for the situation. These feelings are quite natural.

> Please come back.

> Why is she so unhappy?

◀ Nothing's Changed

After splitting up, one or both of your parents may be sad for a while. This can be hard to understand if they split up to stop being unhappy. It can take time to stop feeling sad.

> Why is Dad so mean about Mom? She's my mom and I love her.

▶ In The Middle

Sometimes you may feel caught in the middle between your mom and dad. If this happens, talk to your parents about it. Why not ask them to talk to each other, instead of saying things to you about the other one?

Nobody understands. Nobody cares about how I feel.

Story: Billy's Anger

1 Billy was angry that his parents were splitting up. He didn't want them to.

No I won't. I hate you all.

Billy, stop throwing those books on the floor.

2 At school, Billy wouldn't do what his teacher asked him to do.

What's wrong, Billy?

Mom and Dad are splitting up and I don't want them to.

3 Billy told his teacher that he felt as if nobody cared about his feelings.

Why did Billy misbehave at school?

Billy was feeling unhappy and angry. He wanted somebody to take notice of his feelings. But Billy didn't have to misbehave in order to get attention. He could have told his parents or his teacher how he felt. It is better to talk about your feelings, rather than getting mad or even getting into trouble.

Why do they still argue?

▶ Why Isn't It OK Now?

Sometimes your mom and dad may argue, even if they don't live together anymore. It can take time for them to sort out how to share the things they used to own together. They may also still feel angry with each other.

▼ Other People

Sometimes other people don't understand the situation and may say upsetting things about your parents. However hard it is, try to ignore such comments. Instead, talk to good friends and other members of your family. They will understand what is going on.

Carla, how do you cope with your difficult feelings?
"I still feel a bit angry with my mom but I feel better about it now. It was good talking to Gabriela, even though I know it won't make Mom and Dad get back together again."

Feeling OK

Getting used to changes in the family is not easy. Here Kiko is talking to her school nurse about how she feels. When her dad moved out, Kiko really missed him. But she prefers it now because both her parents are happier. It took a while to get used to all the changes.

Friends can make you feel better.

Are things at home better now?

Yes, but it took ages for us to get used to all the changes after Dad left.

Feeling Ok

▶ In Touch

If you miss your dad or mom, why not write him or her a letter or draw a picture? It may not always be possible to see him or her, but there is nothing wrong in wanting to keep in touch with your other parent.

Why can't I see Dad? I haven't done anything wrong.

◀ No Change

Sometimes you have to accept a situation, even though it may not be what you want. If you talk to your parent about your feelings, he or she will be able to understand how you feel about the situation.

▶ Talking Helps

When parents separate or divorce, there will be lots of changes. For instance, you may spend your birthday with only one parent instead of both parents. But just because things are not the same as before doesn't mean that they can't be just as good or even better.

Who will I spend my birthday with?

Story: Staying Friends

1 Lucy's mom and dad had split up. Lucy didn't want to see or talk to her mom.

2 Lucy's dad tried to understand why Lucy was so mad at her mom.

3 Lucy's dad persuaded Lucy to talk to her mom. It made her feel better.

Why did Lucy feel better after she had talked to her mom?

Lucy was upset that her mom had left her dad. Speaking to her mom on the telephone didn't make all of her angry and upset feelings go away, but she was glad she had spoken to her mom. A divorce or separation is upsetting for everyone, but bit by bit, sad feelings do go away as you get used to a new situation.

▶ It's OK To Feel Happy

If one or both of your parents are feeling sad you may think that you shouldn't enjoy yourself. It may take a while for your parents to feel OK again, but that doesn't mean that they don't want you to have fun.

◀ It's OK To Feel Sad

If your parents split up, you may feel very confused and unhappy. Hiding your feelings can make everything seem even worse. It helps to talk to friends whose parents have also split up or to a close friend whom you trust.

Kiko, what helped you to feel OK?

"When Mom and Dad separated, I felt lonely so I told my best friend at school. When I felt unhappy, she and my other friend cheered me up. It helped, too, to keep doing the things I always did before, like playing in the basketball team."

Don't Forget...

1

What is your advice to someone whose parents are splitting up, Carla?

"Talk to your parents about your angry or sad feelings, and any other feelings, too! Then your mom and dad will understand better how you feel. Talk to teachers and friends, too. It's not easy, but you do begin to feel better after a while."

2

Was it hard for you when your parents split up, Kieron?

"Yes, but I also understood how it made my parents feel. They didn't want to make me sad. Moms and dads have to sort out what is right for them and for you, even if that means that you may all feel upset for a while. If your parents do separate or get a divorce, they are still your mom and dad. Nothing can change that."

3

Did it take you long to feel better, Kiko?

"Quite a long time. Sometimes I still miss seeing my dad every day, but it's much better now because there is no more shouting. I think it helps to keep doing the things that you usually do, like playing with friends or visiting your favorite places."

4

How do you feel about not seeing your dad, Adam?

"It was really hard at first, but I'm not going to let it stop me from having a good time, because that wouldn't help Mom either. I quite like it now, with just me and Mom. And lots of friends, too!"

Find Out More About Divorce

Helpful Addresses and Phone Numbers

Talking about problems can really help. If you can't talk to someone close to you, then try ringing one of these organizations:

Childhelp USA
15757 N. 78th Street
Scottsdale, Arizona 85260 USA
Helpline: 1-800-422-4453
www.childhelpusa.org

Children's Rights Council
6200 Editors Park Drive
Suite 103
Hyattsville, MD 20782
USA
Tel: (301) 559-3120
www.gocrc.com

DivorceCare for Kids
PO Box 1739
Wake Forest, NC 27588 USA
Tel: 800-489-7778
www.dc4k.org

Kids Help Phone
300-439 University Avenue
Toronto, Ontario M5G 1Y8
Canada
Helpline: 1-800-668-6868
www.kidshelpphone.ca

Kids in the Middle
121 West Monroe Avenue
Kirkwood, MO 63122
USA
Tel: (314) 909-9922

On the Web

These websites are also helpful. You can get in touch with some of them using email:

www.bonusfamilies.com

www.familieschange.ca

www.itsnotyourfault.org/

www.kidsinthemiddle.org

www.kidsturn.org

www.pbskids.org/itsmylife/

Further Reading

If you want to read more about divorce and separation, try:

How Can I Deal With: My Parents' Divorce by Sally Hewitt (Franklin Watts)

Choices and Decisions: When Parents Separate by Pete Sanders and Steve Myers (Stargazer Books)

Two Homes by Claire Masurel (Candlewick Press)

What Can I Do?: A Book for Children of Divorce by Danielle Lowry and Bonnie J. Matthews (Magination Press)

Help! A Girl's Guide to Divorce and Stepfamilies by Nancy Holyoke (Pleasant Company Publications)

Index

Accepting a new situation
  24, 25, 26, 27
Arguing parents 7, 15, 16,
  18, 29

Being loved 11, 12, 14
Being naughty 21
Blame 16, 17, 20

Caught in the middle 20

Feeling
  angry or mad 15, 19, 21,
    23, 26, 28
  confused 17, 19
  happier again 27, 29
  sad 20, 27, 28
  upset 20, 22
Friends 10, 24, 26, 27, 29

Getting divorced 7, 8
Getting used to change 24, 25

Keeping in touch 25

Missing your parent 18, 24
Moving 9, 10

New partners 7, 15

Seeing your parent 11, 13
Separation 6, 13
Splitting up 6, 7, 8, 9, 14, 28

Talking to others 12, 21,
  22, 25

Who will look after me? 11

Photocredits

l-left, r-right, b-bottom, t-top, c-center, m-middle

All photos from istockphoto.com except: Cover tc, 24, 27, 28tl — DAJ.

3, 11, 14, 15, 18, 28bl — Digital Vision. 5, 9 , 13— Brand X Pictures.

All the photos in this book have been posed by models.